PASSAGES OF PEACE

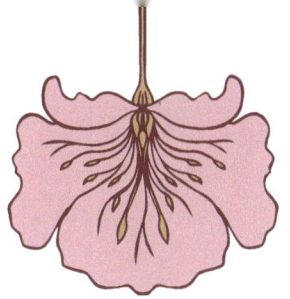

Passages of Peace

Laurie Watson

Art Photography
John Watson
Kristin Boucher

Military Photography
Stephen Smith
Elizabeth Fraser
Arlington National Cemetery

Cover Photography
Laurie Watson

Editing
Jonathan Roberts

Passages of Peace

A Special Acknowledgement

A special thanks to Arlington National Cemetery and each photographer for the sharing of images reflecting the majesty of these hallowed grounds.

The sanctity of our soldiers sojourning presence and enduring contribution to the country is something we will never forget. The peace they proffer is precious; something we must never take for granted.

With hands over hearts, we thank you for your service.

~ Laurie Watson

Passages of Peace
All Rights Reserved.
Copyright © 2019 Laurie Watson
v4.1

The opinions expressed in this manuscript are solely the opinions of the author and do not represent the opinions or thoughts of the publisher. The author has represented and warranted full ownership and/or legal right to publish all the materials in this book.

This book may not be reproduced, transmitted, or stored in whole or in part by any means, including graphic, electronic, or mechanical without the express written consent of the publisher except in the case of brief quotations embodied in critical articles and reviews.

Poeta de Pacis

Paperback ISBN: 978-0-578-21631-7
Hardback ISBN: 978-0-578-21632-4

Library of Congress Control Number: 2018907654

Cover Photo © 2019 Laurie Watson. All rights reserved - used with permission.

Photography by: John Watson, Kristin Boucher. All rights
reserved - used with permission.
Military Photography by: Stephen Smith, Elizabeth Fraser
© Arlington National Cemetery. All rights reserved - used with permission.

Use Your QR App
To Learn More Today

All photography found within these pages are a tool,
solely used to convey the narrative. It is in no way an illustration
of the actual people within the verse.

Logo Design by: © 2019 Kyle Watson. All Rights Reserved – used with permission

PRINTED IN THE UNITED STATES OF AMERICA

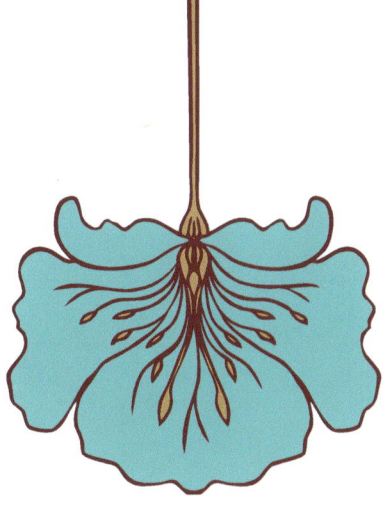

To Bubby, Kristin, John, Kyle, and Caleb

to Marjorie

to all of those that mourn

and to the memory of you, Tommy

Still, I'll think of you each moment
And I'll miss you every day
For a part of you remains with me
As though you'd never gone away

Introduction

These passages of spiritual, or macabre, verse touch on a myriad of experiences, circumstances, and conditions. They speak of the struggles in life, the victories we find within them, and the journey's end.

They express emotions, ranging from raw pain and anger to a calming peace. All are a part of life's processes.

The words within share the many paths we may walk during this lifetime, as well as the inner peace, found within the knowledge that we never walk alone. God is there.

There are no prerequisites for theology or theories. We need not the precise words or even the proper names. His Spirit is both translator and transcriber.

God knows to whom we call. He reaches us wherever we are, whoever we are, without exception.

~ Laurie Watson

Contents

The Dark 1
Angels Always Fly 2
Sweet Soprano 5
The Skies 6
In Reflection 9
The Beaches of
Dun Laoghaire 10
My Sister 13
Hugs and Kisses 14
Dry Your Tears 17
A Talk with God 18
The Walk 21
Love Shall Find You There 22
The Gardener 25
We Glide 26
At Once 29
Joshua 30
Never Doubt 33
The Tender Years 34
Sit Here by My Side 37
A Son Abides Forever 39

A Voice 42
See 45
Chains and Irons 46
Remember Always 49
The Soldier 53
No Words 54
Today 57
Peace 58
My Friend 61
Amen 62
Awaiting 65
A Special Love 69
Utopia 70
The Bond 73
The Petals 74
A Note 77
Sweet So Longs 79
The Battle 83
Goodbyes 86
Always 89
Forever 90

The Dark

Despair reverberates the soul
Resounding its offense
Remain the while within My arms
My peace your heart shall sense

Time nor space nor solitude
Shall cull you from My side
My Spirit knows your sorrow child
It is here your heart resides

Thoughts linger much as twilights chill
Casting shadows in your heart
Lie here within My bosom
And My peace I shall impart

For you're only just a whisper
From the one who truly cares
In my omnipresence
I shall take you from despair

I am peace beyond perception
Dreams beyond your dreams
The binds are not as mighty
As your world would have them seem

So, do not fear the hours
As the night too soon embarks
My light shall guide dream's pathway
You need not fear the dark

Angels Always Fly

In a world that turns with changes
To one truth we must hold near
That of God's unfathomable faithfulness
To those whom we call dear

To this hope, we cling steadfastly
Of its truth, our hearts shall cry
God has shown His propriation
For angels always fly

Their lives blossom into beauty
As time pushes further on
To manifest a sweet aroma
To sing life's gentle song

Then they leave us with a legacy
Which throughout time shall never die
For death itself cannot contain them
For angels always fly

Sweet Soprano

This morning I awakened
To words my heart could barely hear
You sleep within the wings of angels
No longer were you here

We felt a cavernous void of silence
With the absence of your voice
Coupled with the anguish
We were proffered not a choice

Yet we release our sweet soprano
For your greatest aria, you leave
As God beckons you to heaven
To join the angels Christmas Eve

So, spread your wings and fly tonight
For in our hearts, your voice remains
Its very presence stills the sorrow
Its calming sound will heal our pain

For as first light breaks this Christmas
All heaven will sound with perfect tone
For God so loved His sweet soprano
Therefore, He called you home

The Skies

The sky is dark, and the sounds fall still
In the skies over Lorelei's heart
She fears what the future has yet to reveal
In the skies over Lorelei's heart

She closes her eyes to envision still more
Of the laughter and love that once came to her door
She wipes back her tears as she stares at the floor
In the skies over Lorelei's heart

She sits in her chair, so the arms enfold
That her heart not sense what it cannot hold
There is nobody there. She is all alone
In the skies over Lorelei's heart

Her body fails as her heart grows weak
Yet it cannot stop all her soul shall seek
Though others see hope as growing quite bleak
In the skies over Lorelei's heart

Yet her world shines brighter just over the hill
As all she has dreamed of shall soon be revealed
Then kindness and love are all she shall feel
In the skies over Lorelei's heart

Celebrating all that is true to her life
She shall cast away all its burden and strife
She will open her heart and embrace paradise
In the skies over Lorelei's heart

In Reflection

Pressing my cheek against your forehead
I prayed the Shepherd's prayer
You took another peaceful sigh
Then no longer were you there

For you had left behind your struggle
Free from this world's pain
Then within angelic arms, you flew
To never hurt again

As we shared the news with others
There arched a shooting star
As though a message from the heavens
You had reached your home afar

Your journey here was over
Your celebration to begin
 Such a gentle, tranquil ending
For my brother and my friend

Still, I'll think of you each moment
And I'll miss you every day
For a part of you remains with me
As though you'd never gone away

The Beaches of Dun Laoghaire

The sun rose bright so many years
Gentle laughter filled the air
The world, therefore could not believe
No longer was she there

Creation crafted Adeline
Encompassing all that she called dear
Expressing countless stories
Yet it seemed their end was near

She fought against night's tempest winds
That sought to strip her soul
Yet, could not steal the sentiment
Of all the love she'd known

But it seemed her battle had been lost
On that night so dark and eerie
As the frigid waters swallowed her
Off the beaches of Dun Laoghaire

Morning broke as hearts did
All seemed somber and forlorn
Yet her tragedy was over now
Dear Adeline was home

Where peace shall not evade her
And sweet memories ever will
Be held so close to all the hearts
Of those who love her still

"......... HERE ARE NO STORMS,
NO NOISE, BUT SILENCE AND ETERNAL SLEEP."
SHAKESPEARE

My Sister

I'm coming soon to see you
To say our last goodbyes
To gather as a family
To share one final cry

For you my friend, my sister
Mean all the world to me
Heaven knows how much I love you
As I bow on bended knee

Yet I thank God for His mercies
And I praise Him for His grace
For all those gone before you
Are waiting in that place

Where hearts never suffer losses
And you'll never hurt again
You have finished this life's journey
A new one to begin

So, God's speed to you my sister
For joy and love await
As the whisper of God's Spirit
Guides you gently through His gate

Hugs and Kisses

Remember days we lied in bed
With covers tucked to chins
But I must have you rise to face
The challenges within

Not because I want to go
Mommy wants to stay with you
You're everything, in every day
In every task I do

Each morning, you're my rising sun
By night, my shining star
You're everything to Mommy
No matter near or far

None dare try to change the love
Between a princess and her queen
Such love and such devotion
Nothing dares to stand between

My love is right here with you
Though we'll never understand
Still, you and Dad will be together
Reach for him. He'll hold your hand

You'll sing throughout a lifetime
Notes sweeter than the Psalms
Forever and a day, I'll love you
Hugs and kisses. Love you, Mom

Dry Your Tears

I traversed the night within the valley
Ascended, up the mountain high
The gate lay opened there before me
I caught the light within God's eyes

He extended out His arms to hold me
Victory claimed, for it was mine
Never ends, but just beginnings
Providence's path was all divine

I carry each of you within me
Never will you be alone
Angels encircled all about you
Rest your hearts now. I am home

I shall watch the caissons roll there
Hear taps echo hallowed ground
Walk once more behind me brothers
Fold my flag. Let rifles sound

No man could dream of greater riches
Than you have given through my years
Forever and a day I'll love you
Smile for me now. Dry your tears

A Talk with God

I had a talk with God last night
Of realms and diadems
Of those gone on before me
Of angels and their hymns

I longed to waken in that place
Within the peace I knew
A sudden warmth filled all my being
And at once, away I flew

You see, I could not compromise
Who I was to be
I could not stay for you
Without losing all of me

I was born to be of purpose
And to myself be true
I could not change the man I was
Although, I did love you

I saw myself within your eyes
My life, my hopes, my dreams
But God has plans beyond our thoughts
Beyond our worldly schemes

Today I have new purpose
Today I've found new love
I stand upon a higher plain
Time and worlds above

No time for lamentations
I asked, and I received
Today, without restriction
I've not a single need

Healed from all affliction
Strength beyond all time
Because I had that talk with God
Eternity is mine

The Walk

She walks the paths among them
As though they were her closest friends
Extending love and solace
That never falters, never ends

The sweetness of her spirit
Evident within her eyes
Reveals a truth for all who listen
And a hope they can't deny

An arduous tiring journey
Will not keep her from their door
For in the warmth of summer
She'll return to them once more

Giving shoes to guard their walk
And words to guide their way
Offering all that lies within her
Her spirit never strays

She sleeps there, on their floors
Carries water for their meals
Nurturing and loving children
Healing sadnesses they feel

She journeys in the hope
Their lives will mirror old Enoch
That when their time on Earth is over
They too will take the walk

The light that guides their pathway
Reveals the load of which He lifts
For all of those that ask
Receive the power of His gift

Their sun shall rise tomorrow
With the joy of brighter days
As they look up towards the heavens
Whispering softly, words of praise

Love Shall Find You There

Blow a spray of Dandelions
Hold tight Forget Me Nots
Take my hand and walk
Until we reach that tranquil spot

Where discord does not visit
And laughter fills each day
We'll sit and talk till crickets chirp
And sunlight fades away

We'll travel back in time as if
Not a day has passed
For the bond forged deep within us
Brings a love that's made to last

When trees are bare, and winds fly cold
And young locks turn to gray
I'll love you even more in time
Then do I here today

So, cast your stone across life's pond
And know, no matter where
It skips throughout eternity
My love shall find you there

The Gardener

I stand within the garden gate
Immersed within my senses
The Rose of Sharon fills my soul
Liberating my defenses

Surrendered to the power of such
I find my spirit free
Of mundane worries, left behind
Of mediocrity

With more than dreams could e'er conceive
No wings need I to fly
With the beauty of the Master
Everywhere I cast my eye

Within the Sweet Alyssum
Is where I'll make my bed
Upon the velvet Pillow Moss
Is where I'll lay my head

I hear the angelic Bunting's song
And the distant Lamb's sweet call
I hear the soft, hushed rustling
Of butterflies in Buddleia

I bask calmly in the wonder
Of my Creator's arms
Never more to worry
With trifling thoughts of harm

For now, within the garden
Eternally my feet will roam
As winds whisper ever softly
Sweet gardener; welcome home

We Glide

Understand forever love
What lies so deep inside
The heart of the man that loves you
For when you're in my arms, we glide

To places of contentment
I thought I could not go
Yet, every moment I am here with you
I know that it is so

So here, upon life's dance floor
With my beauty and my bride
In time and step forever
Together, we shall glide

At Once

Time consumed his memories
Till most everything was lost
The scourged illness of the mind
Had tallied quite a cost

Where were his dreams of yesterday
When he was just a boy
Why had this villain ravaged him
And seized away his joy

He pondered how the sunlight felt
As light cast across his bed
He longed to feel life's comfort
Yet he only sensed its dread

What more could now be taken
Was there nothing for him here
Then he felt her kiss against his cheek
And his heart was filled with cheer

As all at once, he knew he'd found
What no illness could obscure
For God had graced him with an angel
When He blessed his life with hers

Joshua

No nobler man had met the quest
But upward, onward yet he pressed
To meet and then surpass their best
The child called Joshua

He pushed through every narrow strait
Through lurid gloom and baseless hate
This quiet man, so strong and great
The one called Joshua

He sought not fame nor salutation
But only for the proclamation
Every heart contains a revelation
The man called Joshua

As every doubt, his life defies
His victory stands before their eyes
Be there no disheartened, doleful cries
God says through Joshua

Never Doubt

I once lived for God and country
Born and bred red, white, and blue
Yet never doubt my greatest love
Has always been my one for you

I speak this truth while all can hear
Not when all life's strength is gone
While yet I hold you in my arms
And life is filled with love and song

No talk of world distractions
But children held upon our knees
You remain, my bride and beauty
Hold fast all you are to me

I stood for all of those around me
Not for pomp or circumstance
I stood for freedom and its honor
Not its glory or its brass

For strength and honor built this nation
Transformed this boy into a man
Made a son into a father
Turned a dream to procured plan

The Tender Years

When breezes blew, and time stood still
And laughter filled the air
We ran through fields, and swung through years
Without a single care

For hide and seek and games of tag
And climbing to the tower
On limbs hung low from Live Oak trees
We sat and spent the hours

We stopped to gather buttercups
Or brave through briars for berries
And at the end of young labors
Our spoils to home we'd carry

We skinned some knees throughout the years
And yet we got back up
To embrace life's next great challenge
Our youth had taught us such

Yet now, as time has swept away
The youth, we held so dear
We find that life had shown us much
Within those tender years

Sit Here by My Side

A young girl's heart with spirit's fire
A mother's heart of love
A servant's heart with arms outstretched
Endowed from God above

Her love and loyalty, harbor's home
Beckoning weary ones to rest
Without complaint or thought of self
She strove to give God's best

She brought them to her table
To eat and there abide
With listening ears and open heart
She called them to her side

Tirelessly she rose each day
Weaving every breath with theirs
To suffuse such love, such legacy
Each waking thought with care

But like the beauty of the heavens
Angelic souls must ever rise
Till one day we wake to find
God has raised them to His skies

There He calls them to His table
Sit my child; you've done God's best
You've completed all I'd hoped and more
It's time that you find rest

Come for I have saved a place
Where forever you'll abide
Gather close with faithful called before
Come now, sit here by My side

A Son Abides Forever

Last night I sat in darkness
In my own Gethsemane
To renew my heart and spirit
With the truth of Calvary

To remind me of Christ's victory
Of God's perfect sacrifice
Which allows us to a bounty
Without punishment or price

Had my heart only awaited
And the morning brought new light
I would stand with you my brother
I would carry on the fight

Never trusting in earth's wisdom
But the power of the Word
My breastplate would be righteousness
My loins, I would gird

For, I left you in the darkness
In life's winter, and its night
Morning broke upon your sorrow
Without any hope in sight

I awakened in the arms of God
Though, I leave with much regret
For I see the pain I've caused you
Clinging still to your heart, yet

I extend God's peace and solace
I encourage you to run
The race God sets before you
Wait for morning and the sun

Know life's season soon is changing
And that winters turn to springs
Won't you focus on Christ's healing
And the joy salvation brings

Remember always, that I love you
Cherish all those days I smiled
Won't you hear today my laughter
May it carry you each mile

For its never flesh and blood
But rather darkness and God's light
Won't you promise in my memory
You will carry on the fight

Rise today against the darkness
That God's love instead they see
For a son abides forever
When God's Son has made him free

A Voice

A voice among the silent
Of those who could not speak
A message for the listeners
With ears that wisdom seek

A horror of the many
And yet so few would hear
A voice beyond the silence
Where children walked in fear

No smiles or rings of laughter
The swings and bikes lay still
Were there none to sense the darkness
That every heart must feel

What of the world around them
Was ignorance so bliss
Was it only in the prisons
Where their songs were truly missed

Open doors that hearts may witness
The tears and pleading bids
Of the families of the suffering
As Elie Wiesel did

For history leaves a memory
That time cannot decay
Let us not forsake the lost
Let us not forget the days

See

Some see the tatter of my clothes
The distance I have gone
But can they look into my heart
To know whom it belongs

They see the pain within my eyes
But know not of the cost
They cannot walk within my steps
To discern all I have lost

They look into the very depths
Without a whispered prayer
Gazing at the wandering child
Without courage as to care

Yet among you are those angels
That raise their arms and cry
Lifting others cares to heaven
Should they see them hasten by

Looking there, into their spirits
They sense their greatest fears
Gazing on their pensive plight
They see their every tear

So, I thank those all around us
That take the time to pray
That God lift the cares of others
And wipe their tears away

Chains and Irons

Please do not define me
By the nature you repress
Do not seek through me atonement
For acts which you regret

It is simply a neurosis
Of pasts you wish to hide
A scar inflicted by another
In whom you can't confide

So, you accost me with your slander
And defile me with your words
Their venom pains my very soul
No matter how absurd

So, spare me coy pretenses
To flatter with your lies
I've discernment of your demons
As they wear a thin disguise

But draw your sword to strike me
When you feel that I am down
For when I'm on my knees
I look up to see His crown

Assailed by hurls of hatred
I keep His hope within my sights
You suffuse me with your darkness
I remain transfixed within the light

So, leave in your dishonor
For your words cannot define
A child, freed from chains and irons
By a love that is divine

Remember Always

Mourn today for your loss
But do not cry for mine
For I have touched all that is perfect
I've embraced all that's divine

I left a world in darkness
And stepped into His light
As God held me in His arms
I saw angels to His right

I soared throughout the heavens
And never once saw pain
Until I glanced once more to Earth
And saw your face again

You struggle with the questions
Of cause and consequence
I stand today in glory
Understanding providence

You gaze still through a veil
But I am living full, by grace
I have finished my life's journey
I've completed now the race

There is so much here I must explore
But I know my feet won't tire
For I have the wings of angels
To survey every mile

I will bask in all God's glory
I can hear His angels sing
I've all eternity before me
All the joy that heaven brings

So, please don't speculate of happiness
Had only I survived
For I knew that I was home here
The moment I arrived

Now, do not wait up for me
For I've so much here to do
Instead, live each day to its fullest
Remembering always, I love you

The Soldier

I stood with you in times of war
I stand with you today
Though darkness of erratic times
Leaves lives in such decay

You fight for those so far away
You fight for those so near
You strive each day to heal their world
Delivering them from fear

Yet all conquests are not conquered
Through advance guards and guns
But honoring those lives lost to war
When laid to rest, My son

When there simply are no words
Your presence helps peace find a way
To bring healing to those grieving
That resolute and strong they stay

Understanding all is never lost
For I am in command
I lend My love and wisdom
That their hearts may understand

The path is sure and calm
For they tread upon My sod
Hope beyond the heart of man
I'll bring them home. Love, God

No Words

No words can grasp the feeling
We hold within our hearts
For your laughter and your love
Will always fill that special part

You brought a voice to grace our world
One only you could bring
As sunrise broke this morning
I felt sure I heard you sing

At once, I felt a calming warmth
Envelop me with peace
And I knew that you were home now
That your song would never cease

There among the angels
High within Christ's arms
You are forever safe, sweet child
Free from fear and harm

Forever we will carry you
Here within our hearts
Your song shall never leave us
Your laughter never part

Today

Today our heroes passed away
To join comrades of yesterday
To mount the skies, to take new flight
To build new strength, and gain new sight

Today we mourn the best of men
What higher tribute could one send
Such patriots and loving Dads
No greater honor could one have

Their smiles would brighten every day
We can't believe they've gone away
Yet distance cannot still the heart
And never will their love depart

Always offering an outstretched hand
With heart and mind to understand
And when each trial, each day was through
They sent home words of I love you

They watch us here and smile to see
How very blessed each man can be
With pride and love, we gather here
Holding fast to all their hearts held dear

Peace

What secret to longevity
Kept sweetness ever near
What caused a heart to love so much
To hold so many dear

To give without a thought of self
To find and to fulfill
For the bounty found within her heart
Seemed almost too surreal

Never once had she a heartache
Of which she could not bear
Should any ponder giving up
They'd turn to find her there

To lift them back to love again
To kiss away their tears
And so, God graced their lives with hers
For oh so many years

What pride their lives have brought her
What joy they gave her heart
She'd stay for them forever
But even angels have to part

So, God called her to His side
Where joy shall never cease
A world suffused with goodness
A heart now filled with peace

My Friend

History has brought us many men
Throughout the troves of time
But none of greater legacy
Nor steadfast friend than mine

I hope in time to emulate
His strength and legacy
To reveal throughout my lifetime
How much he meant to me

To strive for greater mountains
To walk that distant mile
Yet, as he did with every quest
To finish with a smile

To lead by sound example
 To strive to do God's best
To live within that higher plain
Where life and love may rest

For history could not chronicle
 The memories that I've had
With my confidante, my counselor
My closest friend, my Dad

Amen

As sweethearts from a tender age
Our hearts were forged as one
We rose together every morning
Slept embraced when day was done

Together we raised our family
As man and wife, we made our home
Each of you have brought more happiness
Than two hearts have ever known

So, I leave you with my love now
And your father sends his too
Remember its foundation
That each day will see you through

May God bless you through life's breezes
Make you strong in tempest winds
Utter prayers, when words can't find you
Seek His solace from within

Awaiting

Her heart a free spirit
That no bonds could tame
She lived in the moment
She lived for the day

She spread love and laughter
Wherever she flew
She harbored the hearts
Of all hurting she knew

No thoughts of the evil
That lie in the dark
To destroy any journeys
Left yet to embark

For no evil could take
What deity filled
No bullet could stop
What eternity willed

Before harm could strike
Her angel was there
He cradled her softly
And brushed back her hair

He caught in his wings
Her very last tear
He whispered so softly
Your Savior is near

Rest here in my arms
I will carry you home
Where sorrow and fear
Have no place to roam

The best lies before you
Such wonder you'll share
For freedom and love
Are awaiting you there

A Special Love

A special love was given our hearts
That shared so many years
The loss so great, it left a void
And filled our eyes with tears

And yet we find it hard to share
What some cannot understand
Until they've known the bond
Between the canine and the man

Races with their people
Walks along the beach
Hearts understanding far beyond
Time and need of speech

A simple sigh of sadness
And they're swiftly at your side
With eyes that speak so clearly
That forever they'll abide

To rest their chin upon your knee
To go where e'er you go
Wags that say, I love you
I just wanted you to know

So, never could they bear to see
That tear upon your face
For all of God's sweet creatures
Are included in His grace

Utopia

Utopia lies within the heart
Upon the hushed slow wind
Seek it not within the world
But in your soul within

Unleash the warmth of happiness
Release the chains that bind
Contentment lies within the path
You thought you'd never find

For darkness hid the beauty
Weeds sought to block its flow
But the journey is rewarding
Love goes where e'er you go

For you, child were predestined
To profit and succeed
It never was your destiny
To suffer and to bleed

So, take the path before you
In all you do and say
Remember, God is there for you
And angels guide the way

The Bond

My friend, your loyal devotion
Will span eternity
Until that time, we meet again
I'll carry you with me

Space nor time can separate
The bond forged in my heart
And though I cannot walk with you
Your love will never part

Each morning I shall wake with thanks
For what you brought my life
To live within that space of love
And leave behind its strife

To hold fast every moment here
Yet touch eternity
To know I stand a better soul
Than when first you came to me

But what could bring such difference
What strength to whom belongs
The outstretched paw, the devout eyes
Found within the dog

The Petals

A life of love and greater peace
Of beauty and of grace
I've found within life's garden
Within its quiet space

Where flowers bud their beauty
And jasmine fills the air
Within each inch of garden wall
I've found life's fullness there

Where all resounds of nature's call
Of birds within the trees
About the pistil of the flower
I've gazed upon the bees

I've known and loved creation
Therefore, the heart of God
The beauty of the harvest
The warmth within the sod

My love for such conception
I share that you may know
That when that last gate opens
I haven't far to go

I apprise that you may comprehend
The petals, for they speak
Of the wonders of the heavens
That its truths, your heart may seek

A Note

Just a note to let you know
At last, I have arrived
To loved ones and to angels
Now standing at my side

I've always sought to capture
Life within my lens
If those were worth a thousand words
Where could I now begin

To depict this world around me
To describe the strength I feel
Were it not for God's own presence
One could find it quite unreal

His timing dear was perfect
For coming is the day
My love shall walk beside you
To give your heart away

Your eyes cannot perceive it
So, listen with your heart
Forever I am with you
Never will I part

So, as the church doors open
Once again be still and hear
Words of sweet I love you
Whispered in your ear

Sweet So Longs

A gentle boy raised on a farm
With dairy cows and tins
When deity looked down and saw
The heart that lie within

A heart that beat for God alone
With love of fellow man
Not to judge all man should be
But loved, 'Just as I Am'

He stood against apartheid
Knowing man could fall
Without the understanding
God reaches out to all

Comforting hearts in Oklahoma
In New York when towers fell
Bringing hope and love to others
With the Good News he would tell

He went beyond the Iron Curtain
To bring peace to suffering there
He stepped within the bars of prisons
To let the broken, know God cared

For whether queen or beggar
The dying or the strong
He offered up the gift of grace
For any heart that longed

He held the hands of widows
And counseled Presidents
He stood just as he was
Wherever he was sent

We share today a great loss
Yet we haven't any tears
Just full and grateful hearts
For all he did within his years

We celebrate his victory
Without words of right or wrong
To God's good and faithful servant
We share only sweet so longs

The Battle

A lady and a patriot
An officer so brave
It seemed her battle never ending
Instead, carried to her grave

Yet she held fast to her children
And raised them up in love
She taught them that the greatest gifts
Are those from God above

She embraced her dear sweet daughters
And loved those once small boys
As they surpassed her every dream
And filled her heart with joy

She lived just as the eagle
She fought to represent
Family, faith, and country
She extended out her heart and lent

A life so filled with kindness
That others stood in awe
For, she lived within the scriptures
And walked within its laws

Till one sad day, the grave news came
Bringing sickness to her door
The lives her heart so treasured
She'd not remember anymore

As time passed by, her mind lost track
Of all she used to know
The memories held so dearly
In time, she just let go

No longer could her heart hold fast
No longer could she see
Through those eyes of greater vision
Of all her world could be

She fought until she had no strength
Though she had not given up
She looked forward to a table
With an overflowing cup

To heal her of the heartache
To free her soul of care
All the dreams that she had fathomed
She knew were present there

Goodbyes

Today we come to say goodbye
To thank you for your love
We blow our kisses to the skies
To heaven up above

We thank you for your legacy
Your life has taught us much
We'll miss those talks we used to have
Your kind and gentle touch

The wonder of your laughter
The sweetness of your smile
You leave a void that none can fill
Of that, there's no denial

We'll miss the wisdom of your heart
The kindness of your soul
We'll seek each day to emulate
To reach for higher goals

We'll build the bond of family
And hold each other close
We'll be there for each other
A rule you valued most

We celebrate your journey home
And every day we've had
In Christ, you've had your victory
So, though we're feeling sad

Our loss is merely heaven's gain
Our saint has finished here
Finding comfort in that wondrous truth
We'll brush away our tears

So, join in hymns with angels
And give your son a kiss
Embrace the joy of heaven
Just know that you'll be missed

Always

Some talk of heavenly sensing
Healing as a soothing balm
I once lived there in its presence
It had a name. I called it Mom

It seems now as though a vision
Of a heart that gave so much
Yet we were graced to know her presence
To find such healing in her touch

Yet some walk so close to heaven
It seems to merely take a brush
And we have lost the sound forever
Of our angel, loved so much

So, we hold tightly to the words
That grace alone can so afford
For though, absent from the body
She is forever with the Lord

She knows how much we miss her
But our needs could not prevent
God from sparing her from suffering
So His angel, down He sent

To lift her up, as she was falling
To keep her body from the pain
And though it hurts that she's not with us
I know we'll be with her again

We'll wade on heaven's shoreline
Talk of all the love we've known
Laugh of how we ever doubted
She was happy to be home

She'll sing there with the angels
Rock the babies all to sleep
Understand how much we love her
Her memory always, we will keep

Forever

I knew my heart had broken
As I saw you sitting there
Without your sweet hello
Within your favorite chair

I knew that I had lost you
Never feeling more alone
Without the laughter of your voice
That warmth we've always known

Still, I know you're always with me
Through each memory I hold
Such love we shared together
No better memoir could be told

So, I release you to the heavens
For you've grasped your final goal
My friend, my love, my comrade
My very heart and kindred soul

I stand amazed that in my lifetime
Of the wondrous joy we knew
Now, remember there in glory
That forever, I'll love you

www.ingramcontent.com/pod-product-compliance
Lightning Source LLC
Chambersburg PA
CBHW041823220426
43666CB00004BA/59